J.H.S.

THE SCHOOL GLEE CLUB

Standard Classics and Folk Music in
Easy Arrangements for Male Voices

Compiled by
GLADYS V. JAMESON
of the Department of Music
Berea College, Berea, Ky.

WILDSIDE PRESS

www.wildsidepress.com

Copyright 1932 by Clayton F. Summy Co.

To the
Foundation-Junior High School Boys' Glee Club 1927-30 whose
loyal friendship and eagerness to learn music
have been a constant inspiration

FOREWORD

These arrangements originally were made for a group of young men who were entirely inexperienced in part singing, unfamiliar with the rudiments of music, and unacquainted with the standard classics which often form the background of our musical appreciation. The problem was to find music easy enough, interesting enough, and good enough to satisfy their longing for musical expression.

The tunes of many of the ballads and folk-songs are printed just as they were sung by the boys in the club. (The tune of "Where were you last Saturday night" is from the collection of John F. Smith of Berea.) The harmonization of these follows as faithfully as possible the straight-forward directness of the music of the mountains.

There are many compromises in the book. Finesse is sacrificed sometimes for simplicity. Wherever possible, the melody is given to one part. The boys who sing that part thus have the advantage of knowing a song which may be used as a solo, if they wish. The range of each part has been thoughtfully considered at every step and optional notes inserted for exceptional voices.

It is easy to organize a chorus of male voices, but not so easy to maintain a vital enthusiasm for singing and a growing appreciation for good music. If this book can answer the plea of harassed directors, "Where can I find music easy enough for my chorus?", if it can give impetus to a newly organized Glee Club, if it can promote part-singing among the boys and men of our land, it will be serving a vital need in music.

Gladys V. Jameson
Berea College,
Berea,
Kentucky.

ALPHABETICAL INDEX

NO.		PAGE
1.	Ah,'Tis a Dream. *Lassen*	7
47.	Ain't Gwine Study War No More *Spiritual*	48
56.	All Beautiful the March of Days. *Hartig's Complete Song Book (1784)*	56
33.	All Glory Be to God on High. *Schumannsches Gesang Buch*	39
34.	All Hail the Power of Jesus' Name *Shrubsole*	39
10.	All Through the Night. *from the Welsh*	17
2.	An Evening Song. *Abt*	8
11.	Believe Me, If All Those Endearing Young Charms. *Irish Air*	18
12.	Bendemeer's Stream. *Irish Melody*	19
57.	Blessed Day of Days. *from the Russian*	57
40.	Blow Ye Winds. *Sea Chantey*	43
48.	Do Remember Me. *Spiritual*	49
23.	Down in the Valley. *Mountain Ballad*	31
41.	Fare You Well. *Sea Chantey*	44
13.	Flow Gently, Sweet Afton *Scotch Folk Song*	20
35.	For the Might of Thine Arm. *Vaudois Mountaineers*	40
36.	God of the Earth. *Mason*	41
14.	Good Night. *Bohemian Folk Song*	22
58.	Go Tell It On the Mountains *Plantation Song*	57
42.	Heave Away. *Sea Chantey*	44
37.	He Shall Feed His Flock. *Händel*	41
30.	Hie Away Home. *Plantation Song*	36
15.	Hundred Pipers, The. *Jacobite Song*	22
3.	Huntsman's Chorus, The. *Von Weber*	8
49.	I Got a Robe, You Got a Robe *Spiritual*	50
59.	I Saw Three Kings *French Tune*	58
50.	I Shall Not Be Moved. *Spiritual*	51
16.	Isle of Beauty. *Bayley*	24
24.	I've Come a-Courting. *Mountain Ballad*	31
38.	Jesus, Still Lead On. *Drese*	42

NO.		PAGE
43.	Johnny Come Down to Hilo *Sea Chantey*	45
60.	Landing of the Pilgrims, The *Jameson*	59
4.	Linden Tree, The. *Schubert*	9
17.	Loch Lomond. *Old Scotch Air*	24
51.	Lord, I Want to Be a Christian. *Spiritual*	51
39.	Lord's Prayer, The. *Jameson*	42
18.	Marianina. *Italian Popular Song*	26
31.	Old Aunt Jemima. *Plantation Song*	37
32.	Old Black Joe. *Foster*	38
25.	Ol' Joe Clark. *Southern Mountain Song*	32
52.	O Mary, Don't You Weep. *Spiritual*	52
44.	O Roll the Cotton Down. *Sea Chantey*	46
26.	O Where Were You Last Saturday Night? *Mountain Ballad*	33
19.	Parting. *from the German*	27
53.	Ride On, King Jesus. *Spiritual*	53
5.	Serenade. *Mozart*	10
6a.	Serenade. *Schubert (1st version)*	11
6b.	Serenade. *Schubert (2d version)*	13
61.	Silent Night. *Grüber*	60
20.	Sleepy Fishes, The. *Old Song*	28
21.	Song of the Volga Boatmen *Russian Folk Song*	29
7.	Songs My Mother Taught Me. *Dvořák*	14
27.	Sourwood Mountain. *Kentucky Folk Song*	34
8.	Stars of the Summer Night. *Woodbury*	15
54.	Steal Away to Jesus. *Spiritual*	54
28.	Swapping Song. *Mountain Song*	34
45.	'Twas Friday Morn. *Sea Chantey*	46
22.	Vesper Hymn. *Bortniansky*	30
55.	Wait Till I Put On My Crown. *Spiritual*	55
29.	Weeping Willow. *Mountain Song*	35
62.	We Three Kings of Orient Are. *Hopkins*	61
46.	Wet Sheet and a Flowing Sea, A *Sea Chantey*	47
9.	Where'er You Walk. *Händel*	15

C. F. S. Co. 2841

CLASSIFIED INDEX

Art Songs

NO.		PAGE
1.	Ah, 'Tis a Dream.	7
2.	An Evening Song	8
37.	He Shall Feed His Flock	41
3.	Huntsman's Chorus, The	8
4.	Linden Tree, The.	9
5.	Serenade *(Mozart)*	10
6a.	Serenade *(Schubert)*	11
7.	Songs My Mother Taught Me	14
8.	Stars of the Summer Night	15
9.	Where'er You Walk	15

Folk Songs

10.	All Through the Night.	17
11.	Believe Me, If All Those Endearing	18
12.	Bendemeer's Stream	19
13.	Flow Gently, Sweet Afton	20
14.	Good Night.	22
15.	Hundred Pipers, The	22
16.	Isle of Beauty	24
17.	Loch Lomond	24
18.	Marianina	26
19.	Parting	27
20.	Sleepy Fishes, The	28
21.	Song of the Volga Boatmen	29
22.	Vesper Hymn	30

Mountain Ballads

23.	Down in the Valley	31
24.	I've Come a-Courting	31
25.	Ol' Joe Clark	32
26.	O Where Were You Last Saturday Night?	33
27.	Sourwood Mountain	34
28.	Swapping Song	34
29.	Weeping Willow	35

Plantation Songs

30.	Hie Away Home	36
31.	Old Aunt Jemima	37
32.	Old Black Joe	38

Sacred Songs

56.	All Beautiful the March of Days	56
33.	All Glory Be to God on High	39
34.	All Hail the Power of Jesus' Name.	39

NO.		PAGE
57.	Blessed Day of Days	57
35.	For the Might of Thine Arm	40
36.	God of the Earth.	41
37.	He Shall Feed His Flock.	41
38.	Jesus, Still Lead On	42
39.	Lord's Prayer, The.	42

Sea Chanteys

40.	Blow Ye Winds	43
41.	Fare You Well.	44
42.	Heave Away	44
43.	Johnny Come Down to Hilo	45
44.	O Roll the Cotton Down	46
45.	'Twas Friday Morn	46
46.	Wet Sheet and a Flowing Sea, A	47

Spirituals

47.	Ain't Gwine Study War No More	48
48.	Do Remember Me	49
58.	Go Tell It On the Mountains.	57
49.	I Got a Robe, You Got a Robe	50
50.	I Shall Not Be Moved	51
51.	Lord, I Want to Be a Christian	51
52.	O Mary, Don't You Weep	52
53.	Ride On, King Jesus	53
54.	Steal Away to Jesus	54
55.	Wait Till I Put On My Crown	55

Seasonal Songs

56.	All Beautiful the March of Days	56
57.	Blessed Day of Days	57
58.	Go Tell It On the Mountains.	57
59.	I Saw Three Kings.	58
60.	Landing of the Pilgrims, The	59
61.	Silent Night	60
62.	We Three Kings of Orient Are	61

Solos With Choral Background

12.	Bendemeer's Stream	19
23.	Down in the Valley	31
50.	I Shall Not Be Moved	51
32.	Old Black Joe	38
6b.	Serenade *(Schubert)*	13
20.	Sleepy Fishes, The	28
7.	Songs My Mother Taught Me	14

GRADED INDEX

Very Easy

NO.		PAGE
10.	All Through the Night	17
40.	Blow Ye Winds	43
48.	Do Remember Me	49
23.	Down in the Valley	31
36.	God of the Earth	41
30.	Hie Away Home	36
49.	I Got a Robe, You Got a Robe	50
50.	I Shall Not Be Moved	51
24.	I've Come a-Courting	31
60.	Landing of the Pilgrims	59
31.	Old Aunt Jemima	37
52.	O Mary, Don't You Weep	52
44.	O Roll the Cotton Down	46
27.	Sourwood Mountain	34
54.	Steal Away	54
28.	Swapping Song	34
45.	'Twas Friday Morn	46
22.	Vesper Hymn	30
29.	Weeping Willow	35
62.	We Three Kings of Orient Are	61

Easy

NO.		PAGE
56.	All Beautiful the March of Days	56
34.	All Hail the Power of Jesus' Name	39
57.	Blessed Day of Days	37
41.	Fare You Well	44
13.	Flow Gently, Sweet Afton	20
58.	Go Tell It On the Mountains	57
42.	Heave Away	44
3.	Huntsman's Chorus, The	8
16.	Isle of Beauty	24
38.	Jesus, Still Lead On	42
43.	Johnny Come Down to Hilo	45
17.	Loch Lomond	24
51.	Lord, I Want to Be a Christian	51
39.	Lord's Prayer, The	42
18.	Marianina	26
32.	Old Black Joe	38
25.	Ol' Joe Clark	32
26.	O Where Were You Last Saturday Night?	33
19.	Parting	27
61.	Silent Night	60
21.	Song of the Volga Boatmen	29
8.	Stars of the Summer Night	15
46.	Wet Sheet and a Flowing Sea, A	47

Medium

NO.		PAGE
1.	Ah, 'Tis a Dream	7
47.	Ain't Gwine Study War No More	48
33.	All Glory be to God on High	39
2.	An Evening Song	8
11.	Believe Me, If All Those Endearing	18
12.	Bendemeer's Stream	19
35.	For the Might of Thine Arm	40
14.	Good Night	22
37.	He Shall Feed His Flock	41
15.	Hundred Pipers, The	22
59.	I Saw Three Kings	58
4.	Linden Tree, The	9
53.	Ride On, King Jesus	53
5.	Serenade *(Mozart)*	10
6.	Serenade *(Schubert)*	11-13
20.	Sleepy Fishes, The	28
7.	Songs My Mother Taught Me	14
55.	Wait Till I Put On My Crown	55
9.	Where'er You Walk	15

THE SCHOOL GLEE CLUB

Ah, 'Tis a Dream

EDUARD LASSEN
1830-1904

C.F.S.Co. 2841 Copyright 1932 by Clayton F. Summy Co.

An Evening Song

FRANZ ABT
1819 - 1885

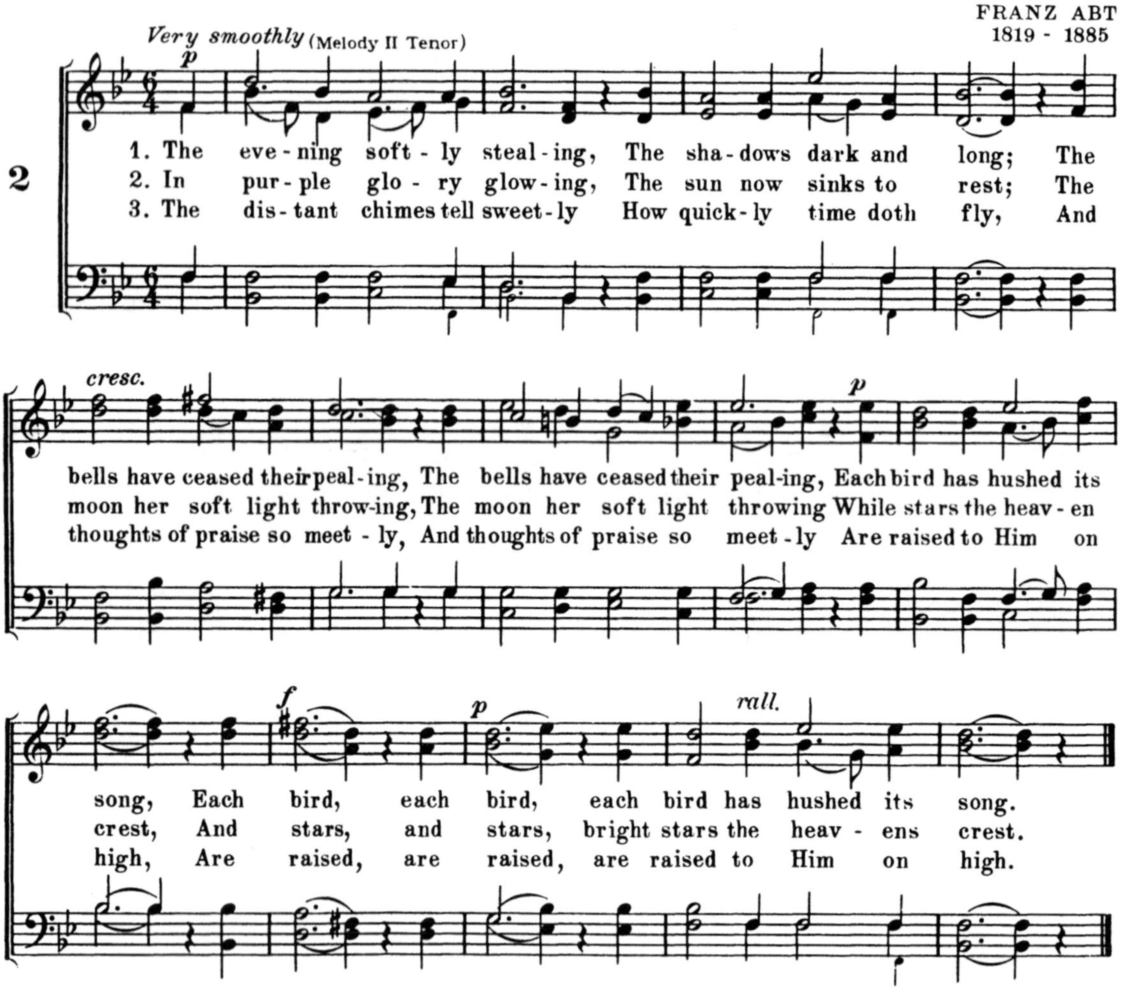

2

Very smoothly (Melody II Tenor)

1. The evening softly stealing, The shadows dark and long; The bells have ceased their pealing, The bells have ceased their pealing, Each bird has hushed its song, Each bird, each bird, each bird has hushed its song.
2. In purple glory glowing, The sun now sinks to rest; The moon her soft light throwing, The moon her soft light throwing While stars the heaven crest, And stars, and stars, bright stars the heavens crest.
3. The distant chimes tell sweetly How quickly time doth fly, And thoughts of praise so meetly, And thoughts of praise so meetly Are raised to Him on high, Are raised, are raised, are raised to Him on high.

The Huntsman's Chorus

CARL MARIA VON WEBER
1786 - 1826

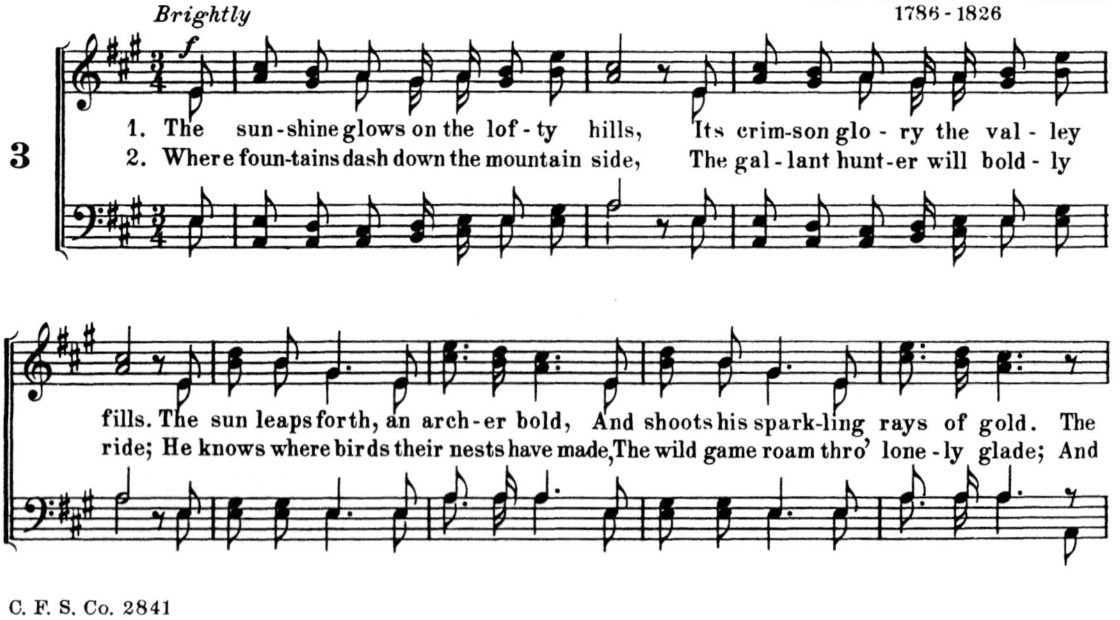

3

Brightly

1. The sunshine glows on the lofty hills, Its crimson glory the valley fills. The sun leaps forth, an archer bold, And shoots his sparkling rays of gold. The
2. Where fountains dash down the mountain side, The gallant hunter will boldly ride; He knows where birds their nests have made, The wild game roam thro' lonely glade; And

C. F. S. Co. 2841

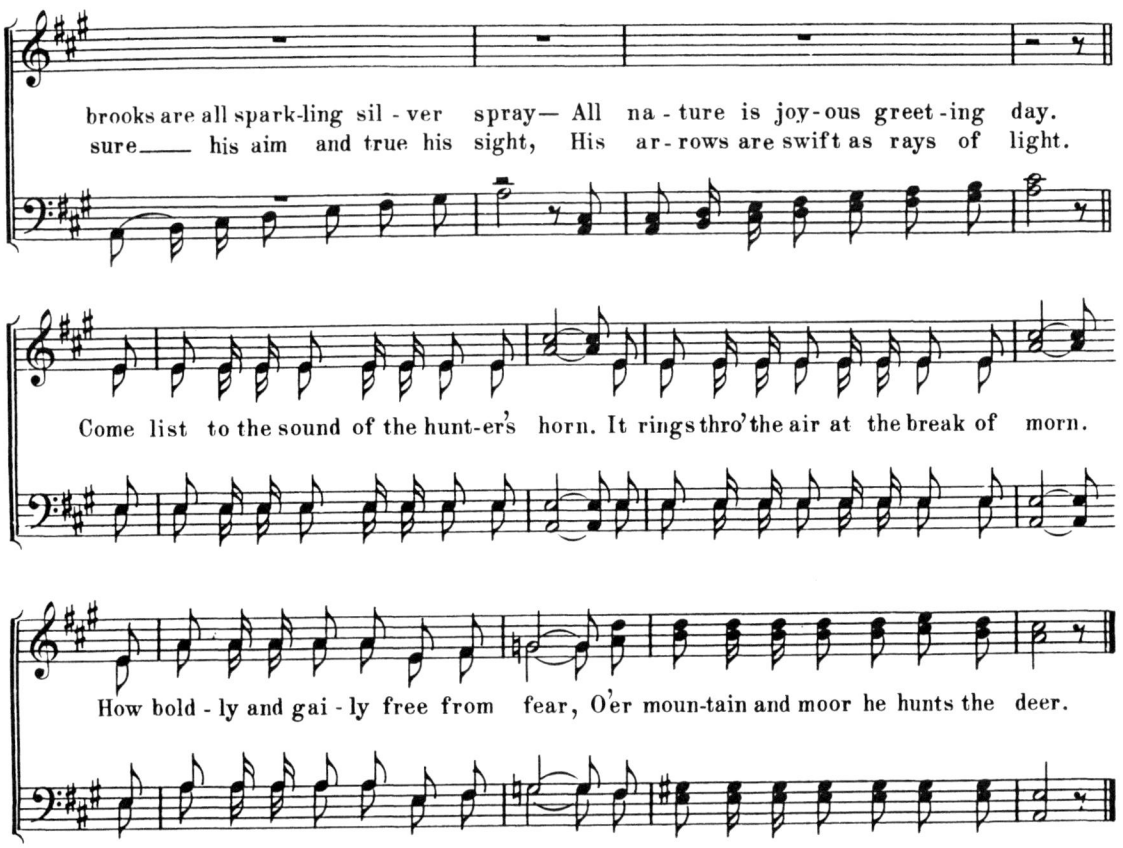

The Linden Tree

From the German of Wilhelm Müller, 1794-1827

FRANZ SCHUBERT
1797 - 1828

Moderato (Melody II Tenor)

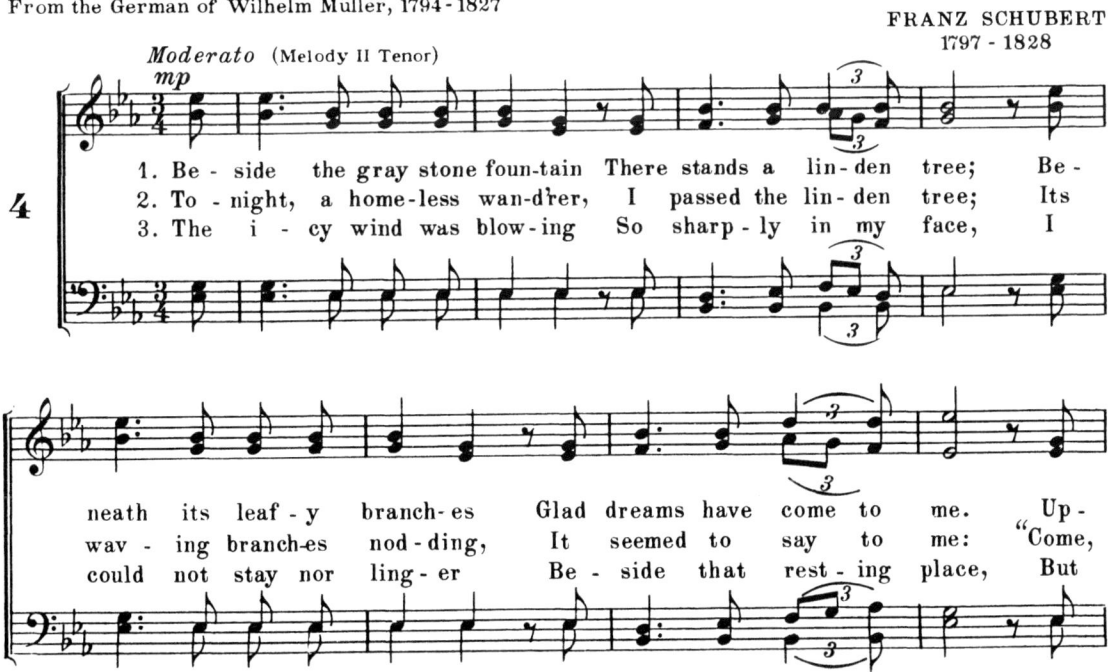

1. Be - side the gray stone foun-tain There stands a lin - den tree; Be-neath its leaf - y branch-es Glad dreams have come to me. Up-
2. To - night, a home-less wan-d'rer, I passed the lin - den tree; Its wav - ing branch-es nod-ding, It seemed to say to me: "Come,
3. The i - cy wind was blow-ing So sharp-ly in my face, I could not stay nor ling - er Be - side that rest-ing place, But

C. F. S. Co. 2841

10

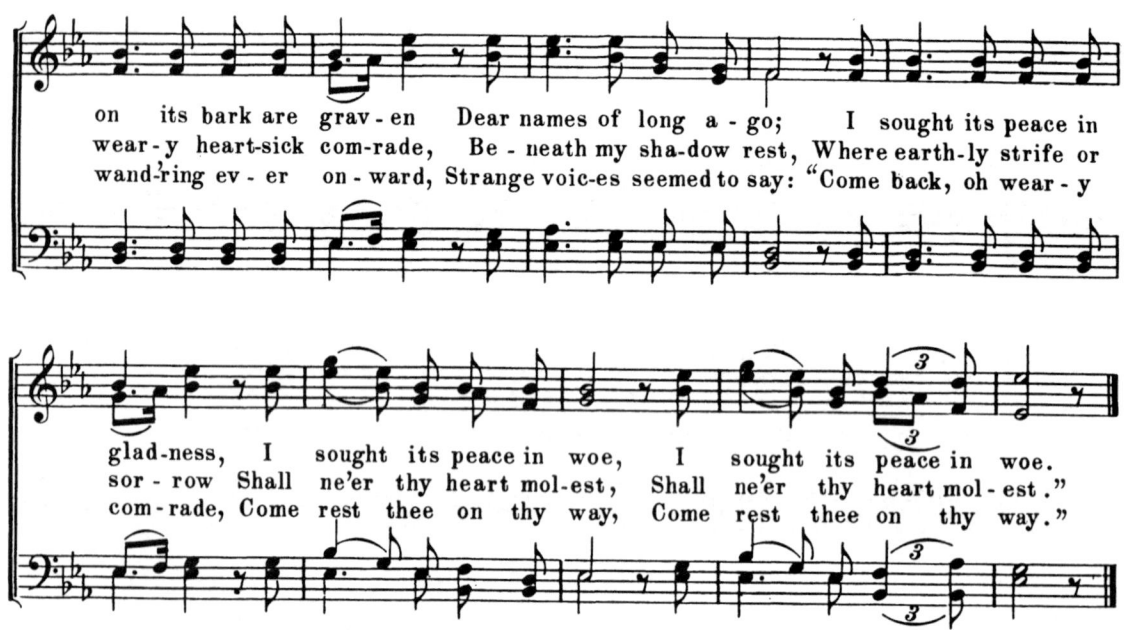

Serenade

G.V.J.

WOLFGANG AMADEUS MOZART
1756-1791

C. F. S. Co. 2841

Serenade

LUDWIG RELLSTAB
1799 - 1860

FRANZ SCHUBERT

C. F. S. Co. 2841

12

C. F. S. Co. 2841

16

17

All Through The Night

From the Welsh

10

1. Sleep, my love and peace at-tend thee, All thro' the night,
Guar-dian an-gels God will send thee, All through the night.
Soft the drow-sy hours are creep-ing, Hill and vale in slum-ber steep-ing,
I my lov-ing vig-il keep-ing All through the night.

2. While the moon her watch is keep-ing, All thro' the night,
While the wea-ry world is sleep-ing, All through the night,
O'er thy spir-it gent-ly steal-ing, Vis-ions of de-light re-veal-ing,
Breathes a pure and ho-ly feel-ing, All through the night.

C. F. S. Co. 2841

Bendemeer's Stream

THOMAS MOORE
Irish Melody

20

Flow Gently, Sweet Afton

ROBERT BURNS
1759-1796

Scotch Folk Song

13

1. Flow gent-ly, sweet Af-ton, a-mong thy green braes. Flow gent-ly; I'll sing thee a song in thy praise. My Ma-ry's a-
2. Thy crys-tal stream, Af-ton, how love-ly it glides, And winds by the cot where my Ma-ry re-sides; There, oft, as mild

C. F. S. Co. 2841

Good Night

From "Twenty-two Bohemian Folk Songs" collected by Dr. Vincent Pisek. Used by permission.

The Hundred Pipers

Parting

From the German

Song of the Volga Boatmen

Russian Folk Song

Vesper Hymn

THOMAS MOORE
DIMITRI STEPANOVITCH BORTNIANSKY
1752-1825

C. F. S. Co. 2841

Down in the Valley

Slowly

Mountain Ballad
Knott County, Kentucky

23

1. Down in the valley, the valley so low,
   Hang your head over, hear the winds blow.
   Hear the winds blow, dear, hear the winds blow,
   Hang your head over, hear the winds blow.
2. Roses love sunshine, violets love dew,
   Angels in heaven know I love you.
   Know I love you dear, know I love you,
   Angels in heaven know I love you.
3. Write me a letter containing three lines,
   Answer my question, say you'll be mine.
   Say you'll be mine, dear, say you'll be mine,
   Answer my question, say you'll be mine.
4. Build me a castle a hundred feet high,
   That I may see her as she goes by.
   As she goes by, dear, as she goes by,
   That I may see her as she goes by.

*All parts except II Tenor may be hummed.

I've Come a-Courting

Mountain Ballad
North Carolina

Ad libitum   *Slowly*

24

1. Kind miss, I've come, I've come a-courting, Oh, dear me!
   I've come a-courting, not a-sporting, Oh, dear me!
2. I have a ring worth many a shilling, Oh, dear me!
   And you may wear it if you're willing. Oh, dear me!
3. They called the dogs and set them on me, Oh, dear me!
   And my, oh my, how they did run me. Oh, dear me!
4. Then I'll go off, and you'll be sorry, Oh, dear me!
   I'll go away, and you'll be sorry. Oh, dear me!

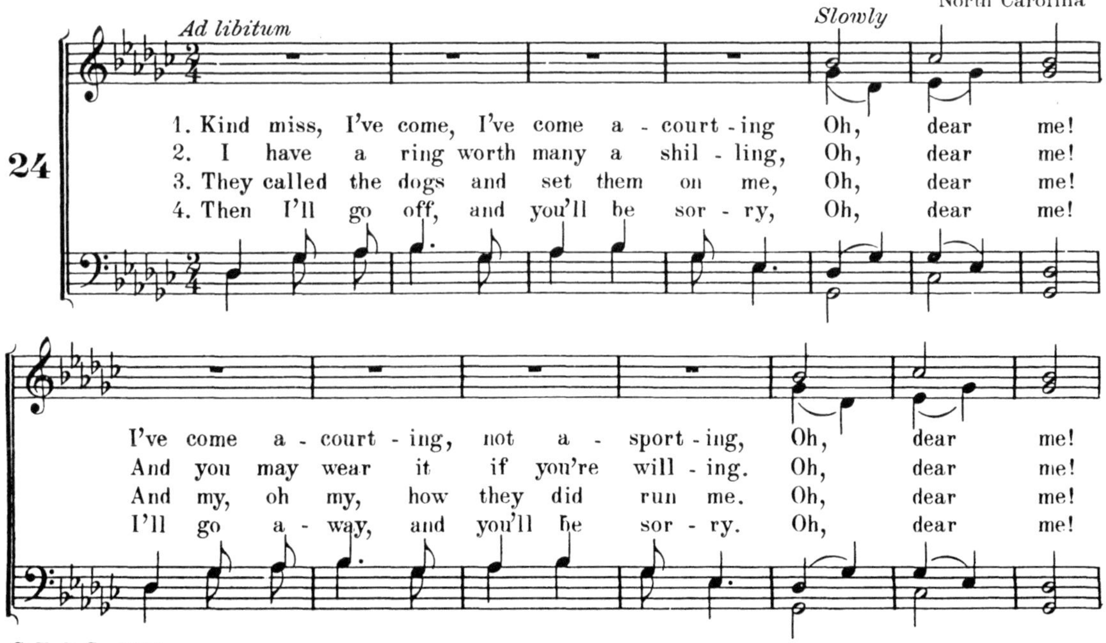

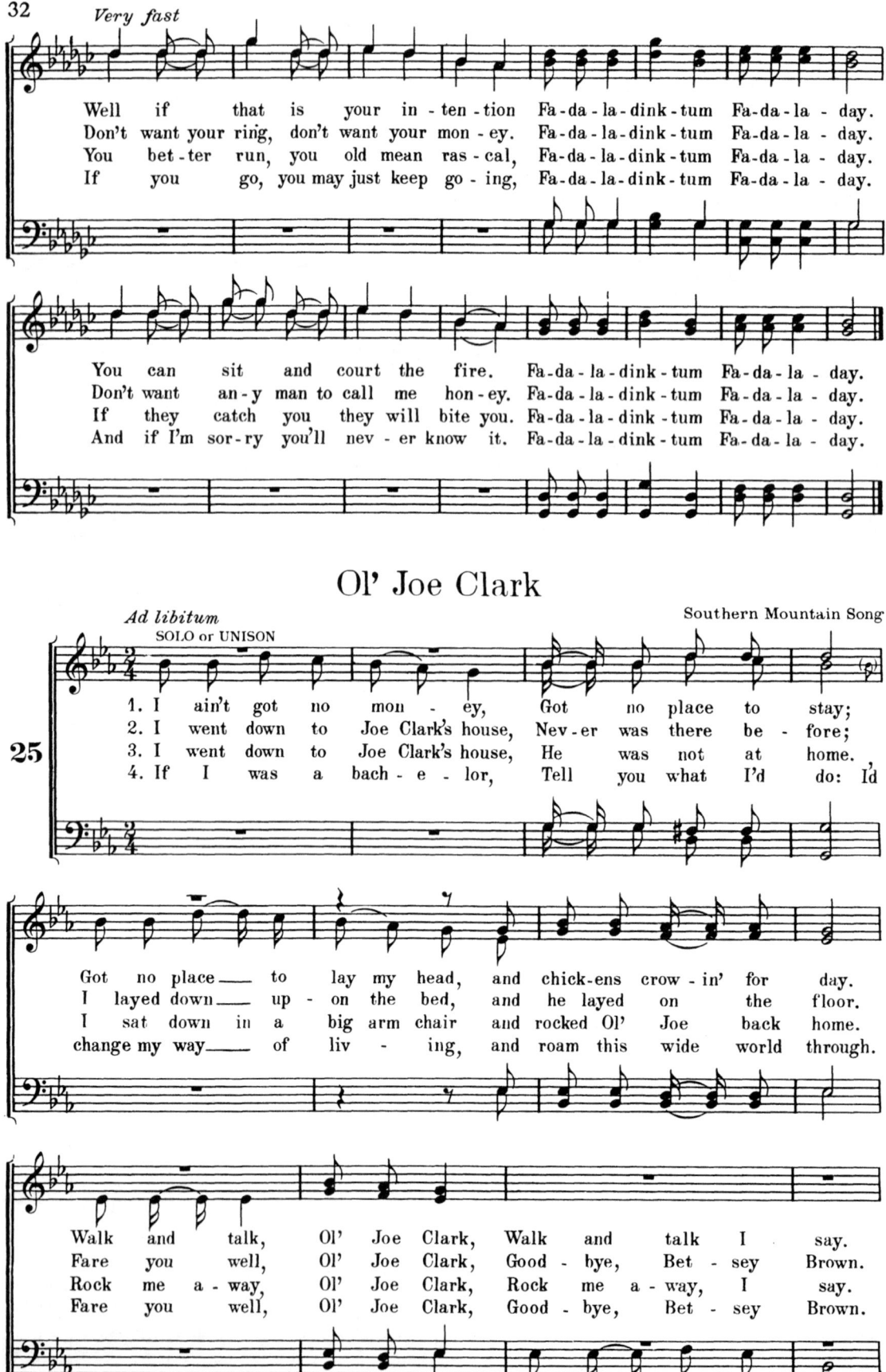

Walk and talk, Ol' Joe Clark, I ain't got long to stay.
Fare you well, Ol' Joe Clark, I'm goin' to leave this town.
Rock me a-way, Ol' Joe Clark, Rock me a-way, I say.
Fare you well, Ol' Joe Clark, I'm goin' to leave this town.

O Where Were You Last Saturday Night?

Lively (ad libitum) — Mountain Ballad

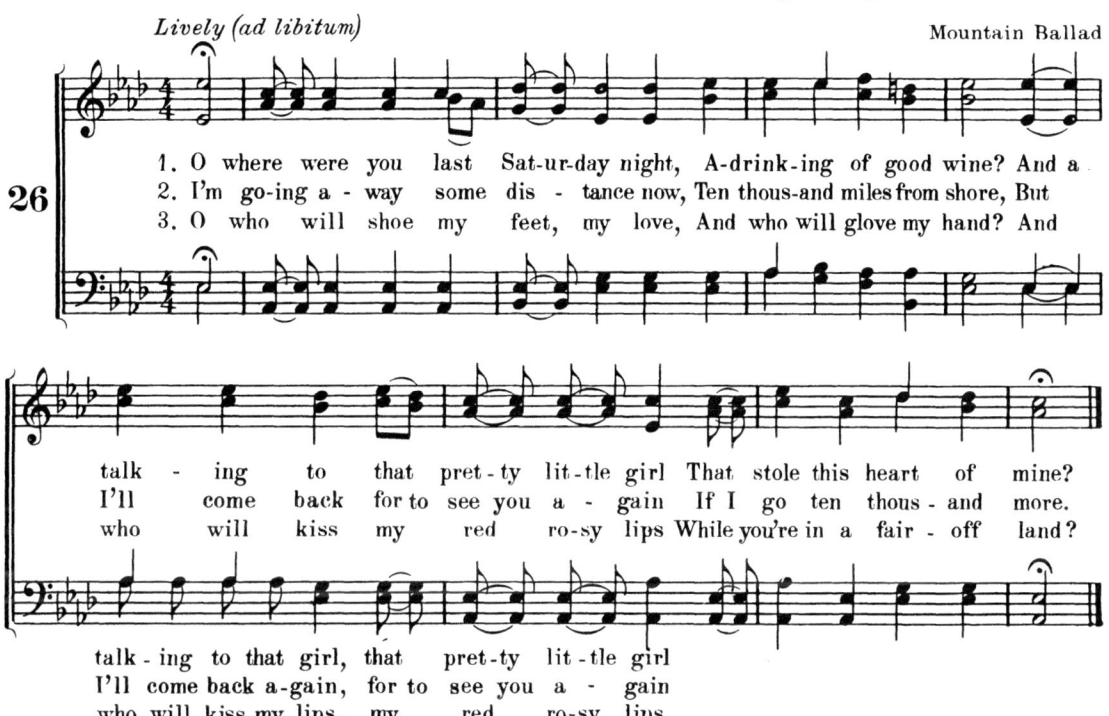

26

1. O where were you last Sat-ur-day night, A-drink-ing of good wine? And a talk-ing to that pret-ty lit-tle girl That stole this heart of mine?
2. I'm go-ing a-way some dis-tance now, Ten thous-and miles from shore, But I'll come back for to see you a-gain If I go ten thous-and more.
3. O who will shoe my feet, my love, And who will glove my hand? And who will kiss my red ro-sy lips While you're in a fair-off land?

(lower voice:)
talk-ing to that girl, that pret-ty lit-tle girl
I'll come back a-gain, for to see you a-gain
who will kiss my lips, my red ro-sy lips

4. Your pa will shoe your feet, my love,
   Your ma will glove your hand,
   And I will kiss (your lips) your red rosy lips
   When I come from that fair-off land.

5. Go saddle for me the speedy beast,
   Go saddle for me the brown.
   Go saddle for me (my horse) the swiftest horse
   That ever put foot on ground.

6. I'll ride away at the break of day,
   I'll ride down to the sea,
   And I'll get me (bags of) gold and silver too,
   While my true love waits for me.

7. So fare you well, my pretty little miss,
   So fare you well, my dear,
   I'm coming back (again) for to see you again
   If it takes ten thousand year.

C. F. S. Co. 2841

*The first four verses are found in "Mother Goose"

5. I swapped my wheel-barrow and got me a horse,
   And then I rode from cross to cross.

6. I swapped my horse and got me a mule,
   And then I rode like a daggone fool.

7. I swapped my mule and got me a cow,
   And in that trade I just learned how.

8. I swapped my cow and I got me a calf,
   And in that trade I just lost half.

9. I swapped my calf and got me a sheep,
   And then I rode myself to sleep.

10. I swapped my sheep and got me a rat,
    And I put him on the haystack away from the cat.

11. I swapped my rat and got me a mole,
    And the daggone thing ran straight in his hole.

Weeping Willow

C. F. S. Co. 2841

Old Aunt Jemima

Plantation Song

31

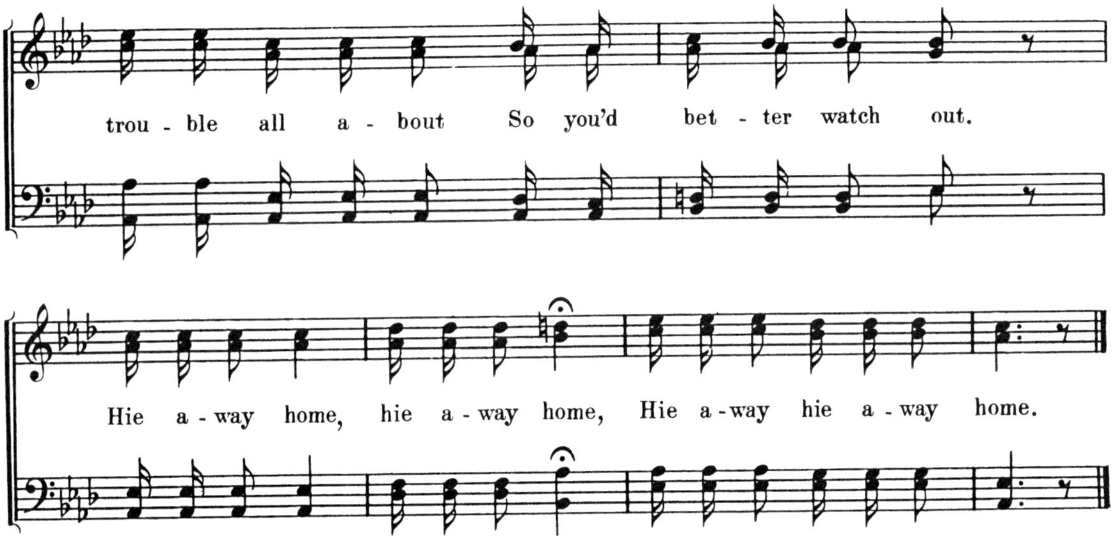

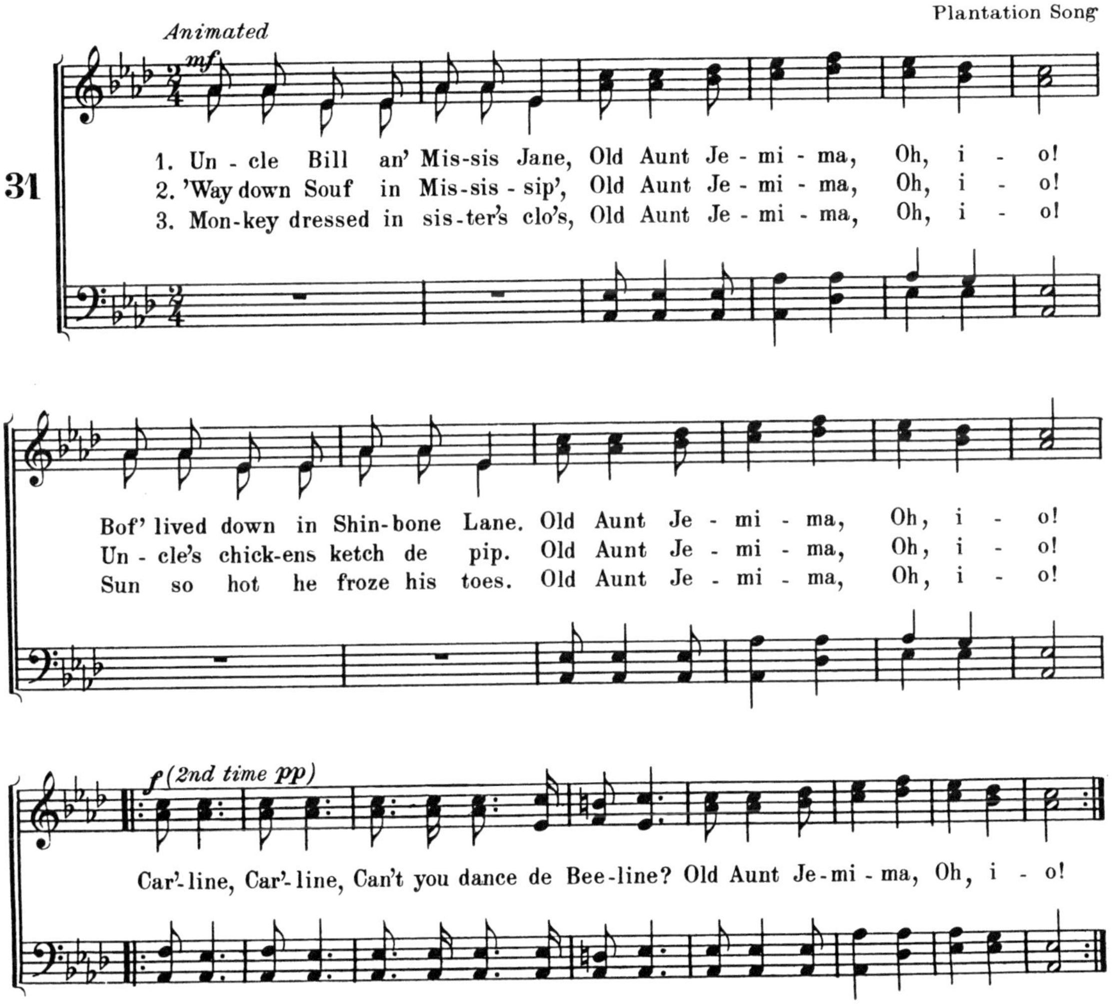

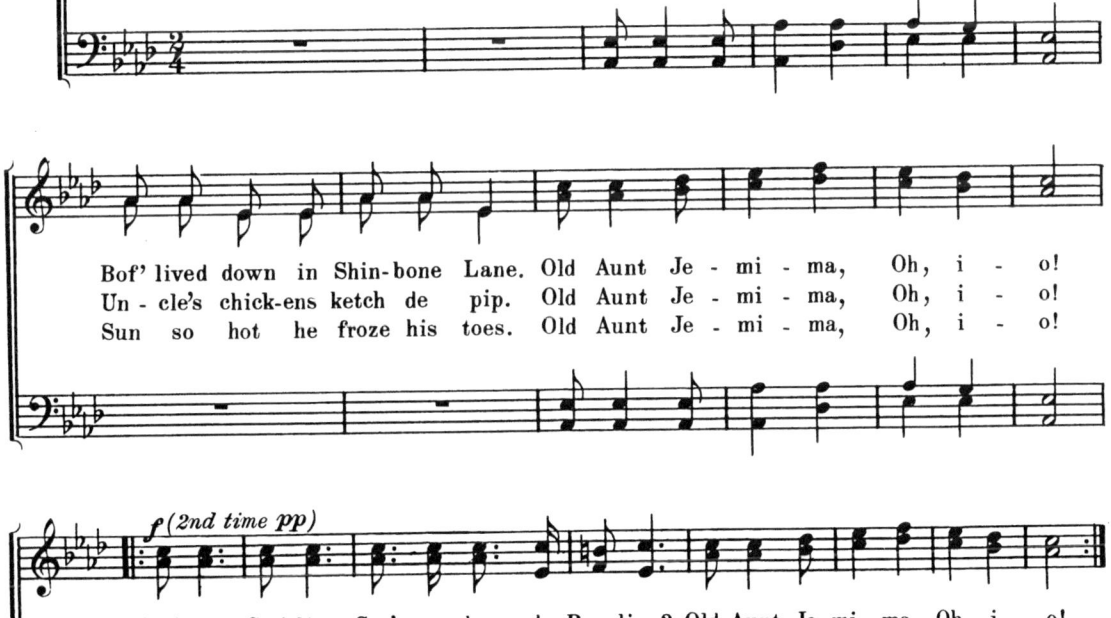

Old Black Joe

S. C. F.
STEPHEN C. FOSTER

32

1. Gone are the days when my heart was young and gay;
2. Why do I weep when my heart should feel no pain?
3. Where are the hearts once so happy and so free? The

Gone are my friends from the cotton fields away; Gone from the earth to a
Why should I sigh that my friends come not again? Grieving for forms now de-
children so dear that I held upon my knee? Gone to the shore where my

better land I know, I hear their gentle voices calling, "Old Black Joe!"
parted long ago, I hear their gentle voices calling, "Old Black Joe!"
soul has longed to go, I hear their gentle voices calling, "Old Black Joe!"

I'm coming, I'm coming, For my head is bending
(Melody I Bass)

low; I hear their gentle voices calling, "Old Black Joe!"

(Melody II Bass)

C. F. S. Co. 2841

For the Might of Thine Arm

C. SYLVESTER HORNE

Adapted from "Hymn of the Vaudois Mountaineers"
by C. S. HORNE

35

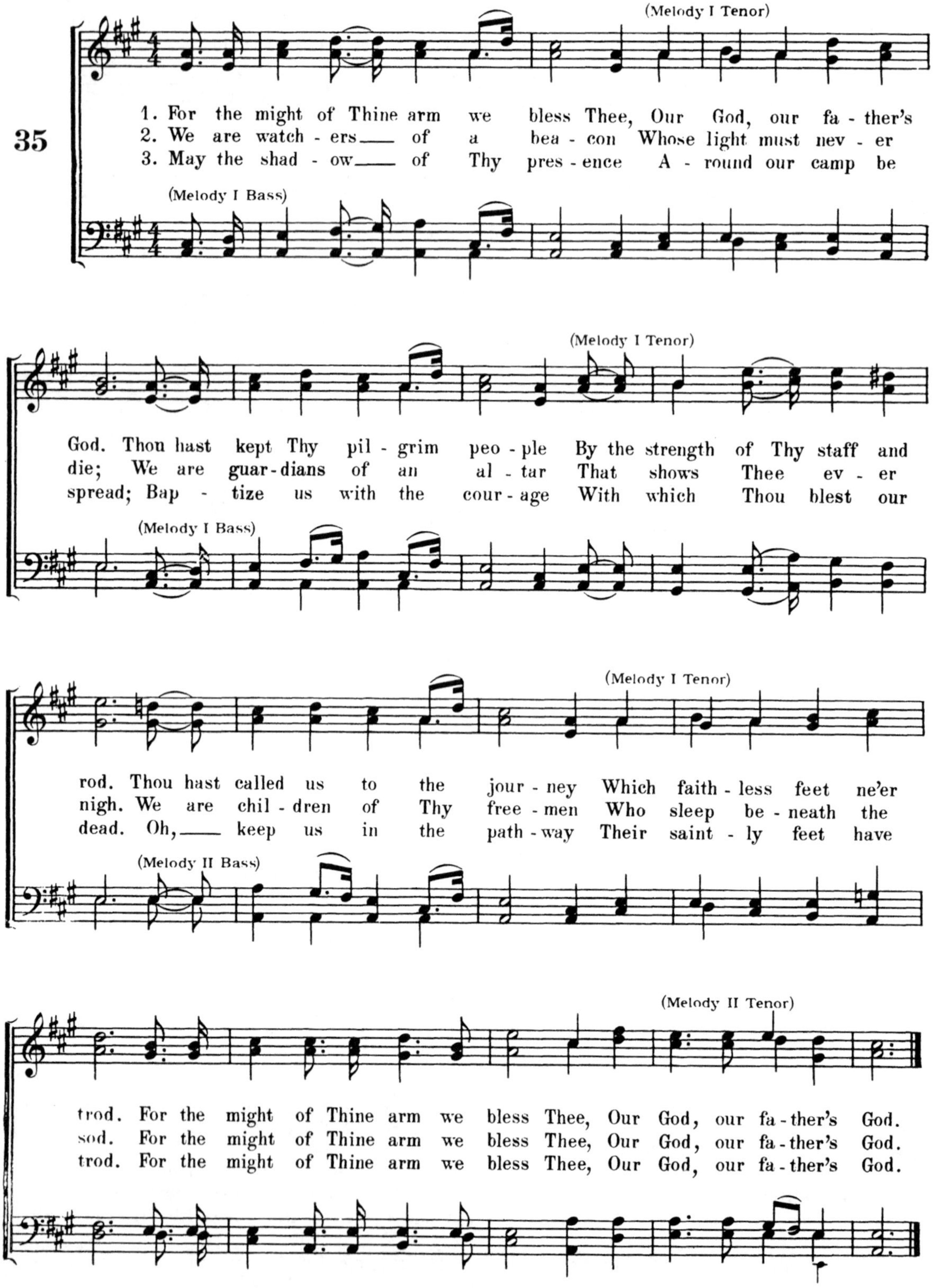

1. For the might of Thine arm we bless Thee, Our God, our father's God. Thou hast kept Thy pilgrim people By the strength of Thy staff and rod. Thou hast called us to the journey Which faithless feet ne'er trod. For the might of Thine arm we bless Thee, Our God, our father's God.

2. We are watchers of a beacon Whose light must never die; We are guardians of an altar That shows Thee ever nigh. We are children of Thy freemen Who sleep beneath the sod. For the might of Thine arm we bless Thee, Our God, our father's God.

3. May the shadow of Thy presence Around our camp be spread; Baptize us with the courage With which Thou blest our dead. Oh, keep us in the pathway Their saintly feet have trod. For the might of Thine arm we bless Thee, Our God, our father's God.

C. P. S. Co. 2841

Fare You Well

Sea Chantey

From "Roll and Go" by Joanna C. Colcord. Copyright 1924
Used by special permission of the publishers, The Bobbs-Merrill Company.

2. We're homeward bound, heave up and down,
   Oh, heave on the capstan and make it spin round.

3. Our anchors we'll weigh and our sails we will set;
   The friends we are leaving, we leave with regret.

4. Oh, heave with a will and heave long and strong,
   And sing a good chorus, for 'tis a good song.

5. We're homeward bound, you've heard them say,
   Then hook on the catfall and run her away.

6. She's a flash clipper packet and bound for to go;
   With the girls on the tow rope she can not say no.

7. We're homeward bound, and the winds they blow fair,
   And there'll be many true friends to greet us there.

Heave Away

Sea Chantey

C. F. S. Co. 2841

Johnny Come Down to Hilo

Sea Chantey

With spirit

1. I neb-ber see de like since I been born, When a big buck nig-ger wid his sea boots on Says, John-ny come down to Hi-lo, Poor old man.
2. I lub a lit-tle gal a-cross de sea, She's a Ba-dian beau-ty, and she says to me: Oh, John-ny come down to
3. O, was you eb-ber down in Mo-bile Bay, Where dey screws de cot-ton on a sum-mer day? Oh, John-ny come down to
4. Did you eb-ber see de old plan-ta-tion boss, And de long-tailed fil-ly and de big black hoss? Oh, John-ny come down to

Oh, wake her, Oh, shake her, Oh, wake dat gal wid de blue dress on When John-ny comes down to Hi-lo, Poor old man.

From "Roll and Go" by Joanna C. Colcord. Copyright 1924
Used by special permission of the publishers, The Bobbs-Merrill Company.

O, Roll the Cotton Down

Sea Chantey

1. I'm bound to Alabama, O, roll the cotton down! I'm bound to Alabama O, roll the cotton down.
2. I thought I heard our old man say, O, roll the cotton down! He'd sail away to Mobile Bay, O, roll the cotton down.
3. I heard him say to Mobile Bay, O, roll the cotton down! He'd sail away at break of day, O, roll the cotton down.
4. Old Mobile Bay's no place for me, O, roll the cotton down! I want to sail some other sea, O, roll the cotton down.

From "Roll and Go" by Joanna C. Colcord. Copyright 1924
Used by special permission of the publishers, the Bobbs-Merrill Company.

'Twas Friday Morn

Sea Chantey

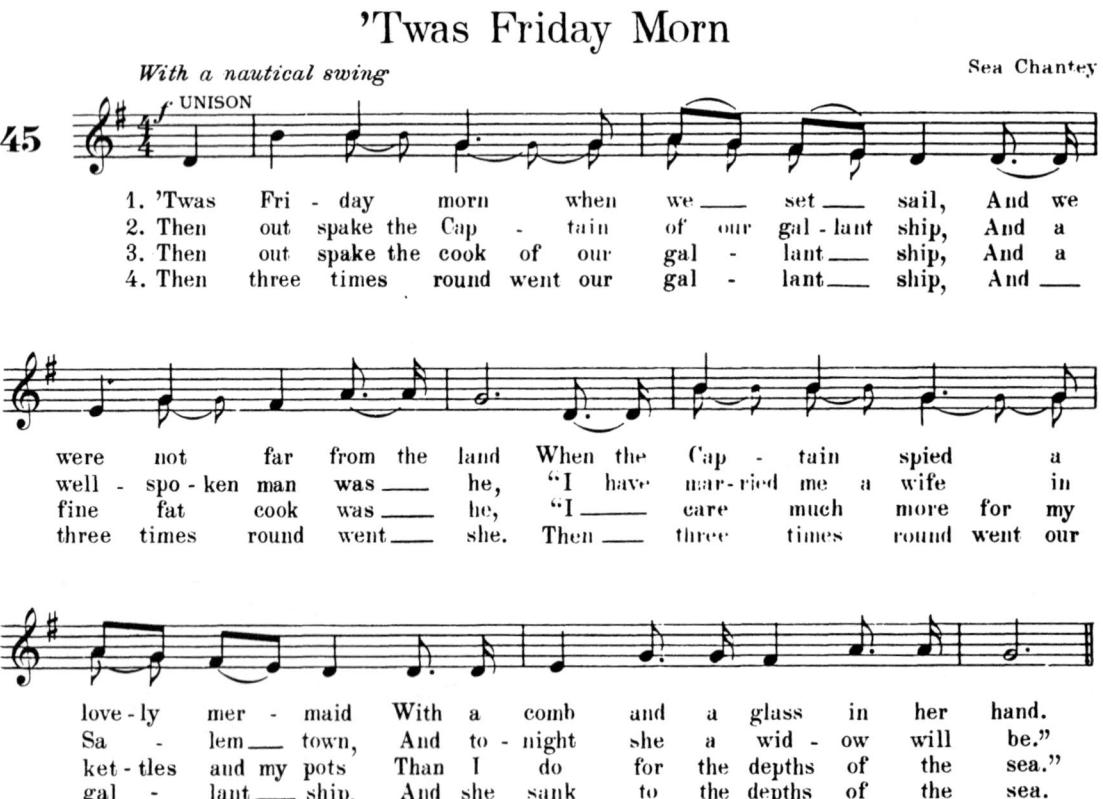

1. 'Twas Friday morn when we set sail, And we were not far from the land When the Captain spied a lovely mermaid With a comb and a glass in her hand.
2. Then out spake the Captain of our gallant ship, And a well-spoken man was he, "I have married me a wife in Salem town, And tonight she a widow will be."
3. Then out spake the cook of our gallant ship, And a fine fat cook was he, "I care much more for my kettles and my pots Than I do for the depths of the sea."
4. Then three times round went our gallant ship, And three times round went she. Then three times round went our gallant ship, And she sank to the depths of the sea.

Ain't Gwine Study War No More

Do Remember Me

I Got a Robe, You Got a Robe

Spiritual

C. F. S. Co. 2841

I Shall Not Be Moved

50

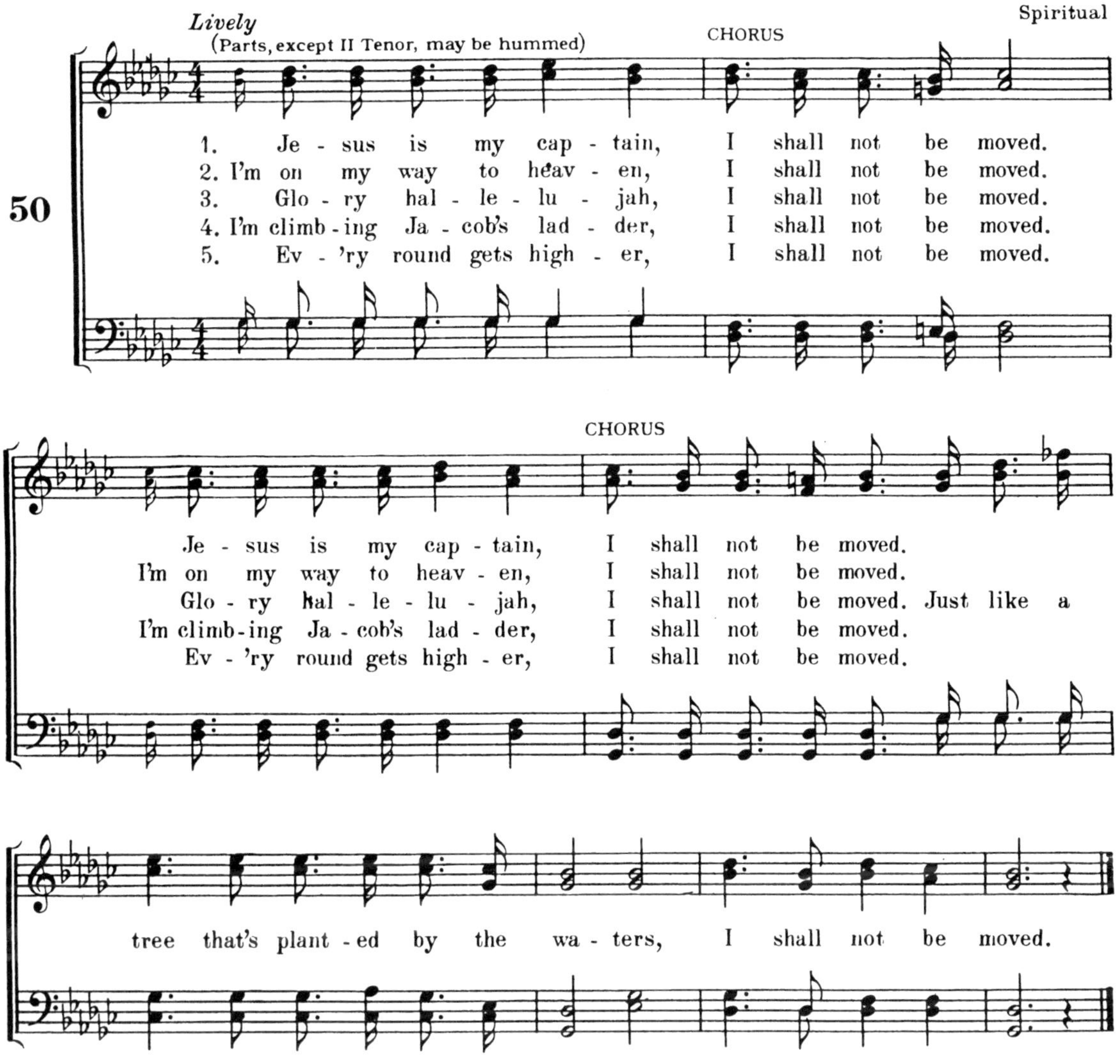

Lively
(Parts, except II Tenor, may be hummed)   CHORUS   Spiritual

1. Je - sus is my cap - tain, I shall not be moved.
2. I'm on my way to heav - en, I shall not be moved.
3. Glo - ry hal - le - lu - jah, I shall not be moved.
4. I'm climb - ing Ja - cob's lad - der, I shall not be moved.
5. Ev - 'ry round gets high - er, I shall not be moved.

CHORUS

Je - sus is my cap - tain, I shall not be moved.
I'm on my way to heav - en, I shall not be moved.
Glo - ry hal - le - lu - jah, I shall not be moved. Just like a
I'm climb - ing Ja - cob's lad - der, I shall not be moved.
Ev - 'ry round gets high - er, I shall not be moved.

tree that's plant - ed by the wa - ters, I shall not be moved.

Lord, I Want to Be a Christian

51

Fervently   Spiritual
mf   (Melody II Tenor)

1. Lord, I want to be a Chris - tian, in - a my heart, in - a my
2. Lord, I want to be more ho - ly, in - a my heart, in - a my
3. I don't want to be like Ju - das, in - a my heart, in - a my
4. Lord, I want to be more lov - in', in - a my heart, in - a my
5. I just want to be like Je - sus, in - a my heart, in - a my

C.F.S. Co. 2841

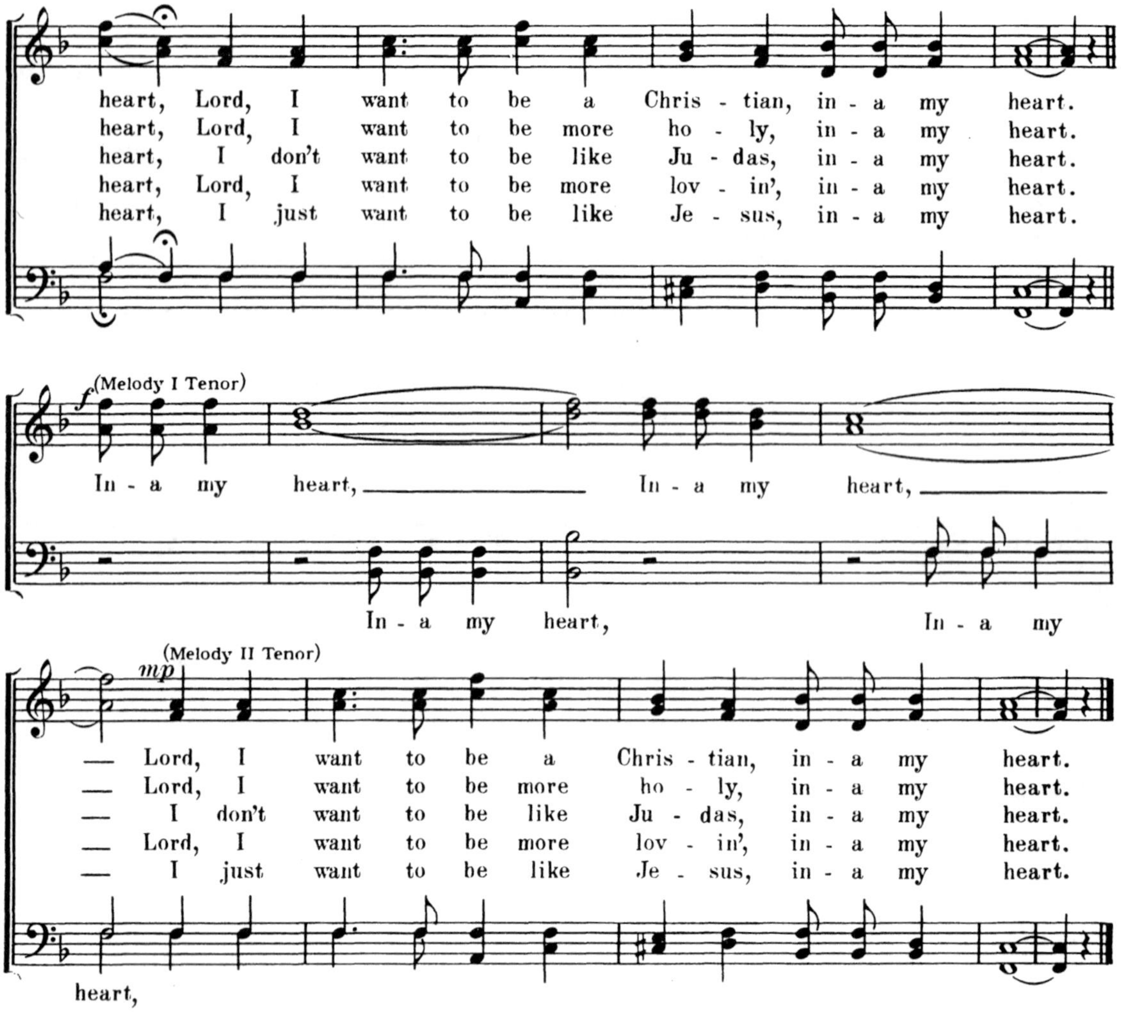

O Mary, Don't You Weep

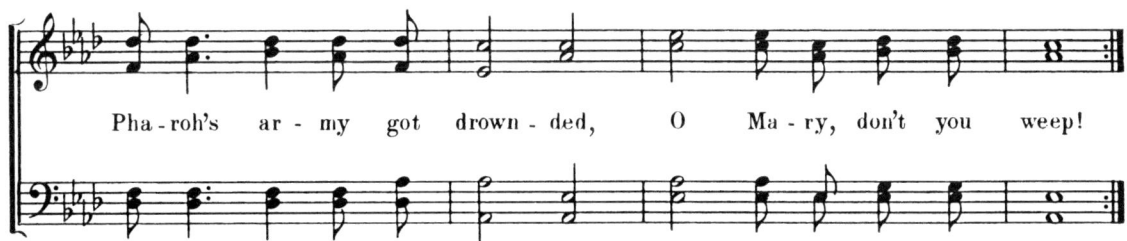

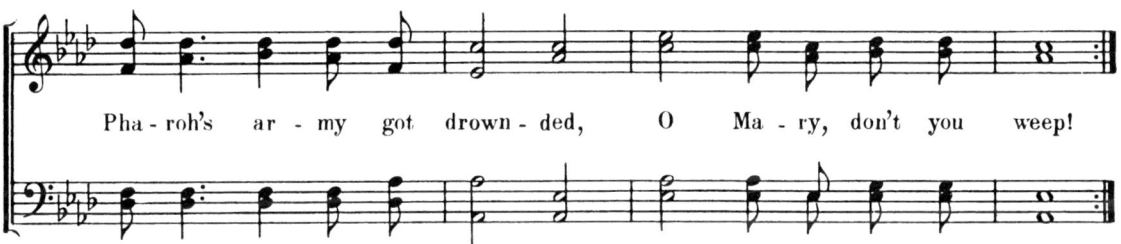

Ride On, King Jesus

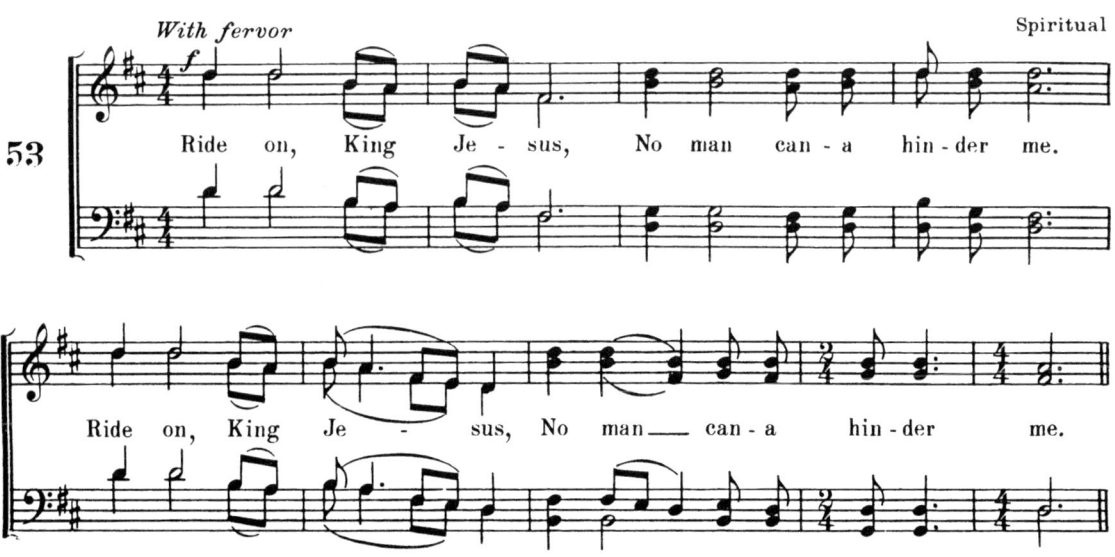

Steal Away to Jesus

Wait Till I Put On My Crown

All Beautiful the March of Days

I Saw Three Kings

Traditional
FRENCH TUNE

59

1. I saw three kings up-on the break of day Come rid-ing proud-ly with a train in brave ar-ray, And as they rode I marked the ar-mor bright That shone like sil-ver in the ear-ly light.
2. I saw three kings up-on the break of day Come rid-ing fast and straight with men in brave ar-ray, And as they came, of court-iers rode a score, With pre-cious of-fer-ings of gold-en store.

And o'er them all as they took their way, There beamed a star that was bright as the morn-ing, And rid-ing fast from the east-ern way, I saw three kings at the break of day.

C. F. S. Co. 2841

The Landing of the Pilgrims

HEMANS G. V. JAMESON

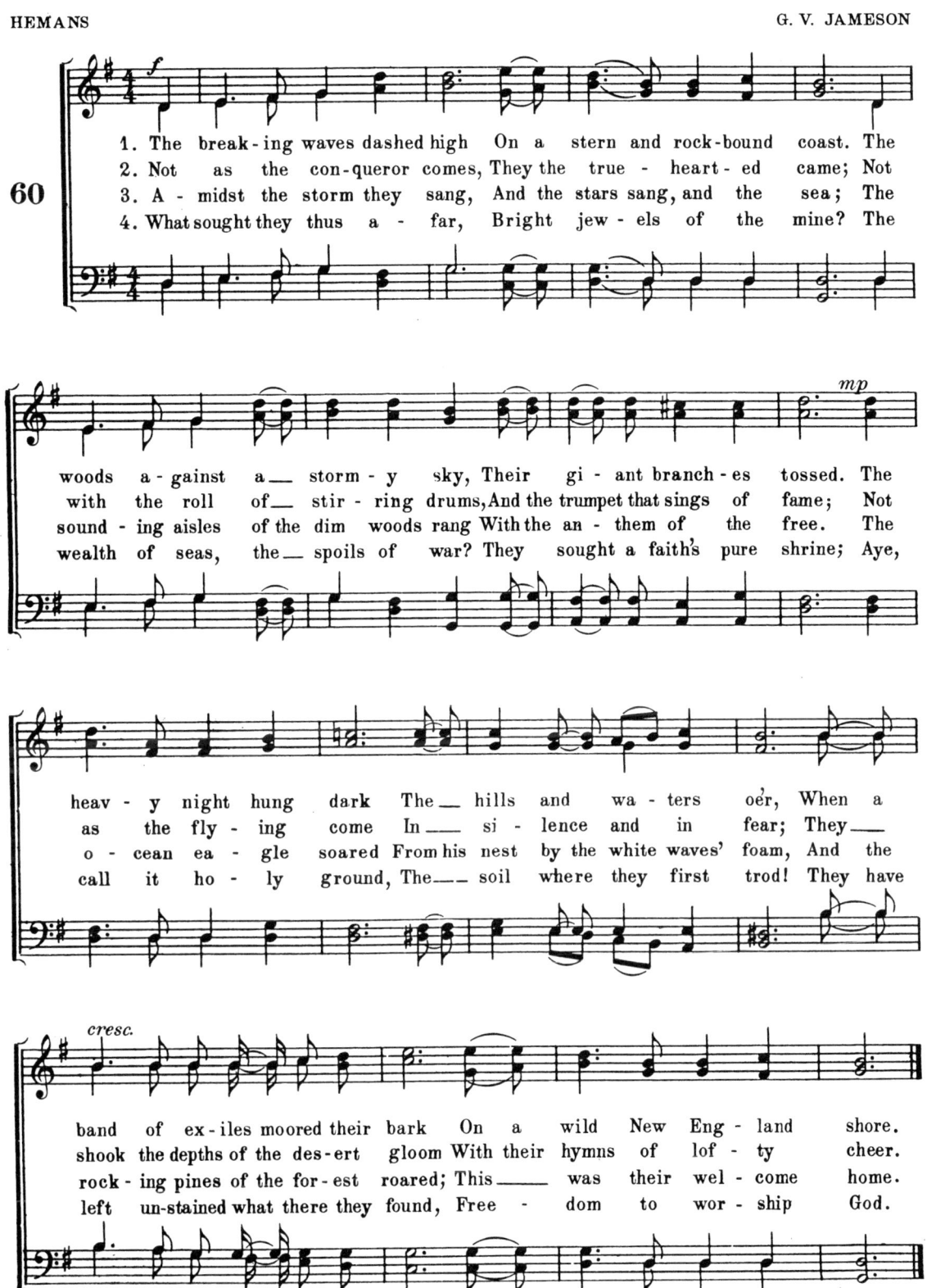

1. The breaking waves dashed high On a stern and rock-bound coast. The woods against a stormy sky, Their giant branches tossed. The heavy night hung dark The hills and waters o'er, When a band of exiles moored their bark On a wild New England shore.

2. Not as the conqueror comes, They the true-hearted came; Not with the roll of stirring drums, And the trumpet that sings of fame; Not as the flying come In silence and in fear; They shook the depths of the desert gloom With their hymns of lofty cheer.

3. Amidst the storm they sang, And the stars sang, and the sea; The sounding aisles of the dim woods rang With the anthem of the free. The ocean eagle soared From his nest by the white waves' foam, And the rocking pines of the forest roared; This was their welcome home.

4. What sought they thus afar, Bright jewels of the mine? The wealth of seas, the spoils of war? They sought a faith's pure shrine; Aye, call it holy ground, The soil where they first trod! They have left unstained what there they found, Freedom to worship God.

C. F. S. Co. 2841

Lightning Source UK Ltd.
Milton Keynes UK
25 February 2010

150553UK00001B/120/P